CULTURE IN ACTION

Twenty-first Century Shakespeare

Elizabeth Raum

Raintree

www.raintreepublishers.co.uk
Visit our website to find out
more information about
Raintree books.

To order:

☎ Phone 0845 6044371
📄 Fax +44 (0) 1865 312263
🖱 Email myorders@raintreepublishers.co.uk

Customers from outside the UK please telephone +44 1865 312262

Raintree is an imprint of Capstone Global Library Limited,
a company incorporated in England and Wales having its
registered office at 7 Pilgrim Street, London, EC4V 6LB
– Registered company number: 6695582

Edited by Louise Galpine, Megan Cotugno, and Abby Colich
Designed by Ryan Frieson
Original illustrations © Capstone Global Library Ltd
Illustrated by Cavedweller Studio, Randy Schirz
Picture research by Liz Alexander
Originated by Capstone Global Library Ltd
Printed in China by China Translation & Printing
   Services Ltd

ISBN 978 1 406216 99 8
14 13 12 11 10
10 9 8 7 6 5 4 3 2 1

British Library Cataloguing in Publication Data
Raum, Elizabeth
Twenty-first century Shakespeare. – (Culture in action)
822.3'3-dc22
A full catalogue record for this book is available from the
British Library.

Acknowledgements
We would like to thank the following for permission to
reproduce photographs: Alamy pp. **5** (© Hemis), **16** (©
United Archives GmbH), **27** (© AA World Travel Library);
Corbis pp. **8** (© Adrian Dennis/epa), **18**, **24** (© Robbie Jack);
Getty Images pp. **6** (Barry King/WireImage), **7**, **9** (AFP), **22**
(Science & Society Picture Library); © Max Summerlee p. **23**;
Rex Features pp. **12**, **13** (Alastair Muir), **15** (20th Century
Fox), **19** (ITV); Science Photo Library p. **4** (NASA); © 2007,
SelfMadeHero p. **20**; Shutterstock p. **26** (© Silas Lindenstein);
The Kobal Collection pp. **10** (Dreamworks SKG), **11**
(Paramount), **17** (MGM).

Cover photograph of Juliet from Baz Luhrmann's 1996 film
Romeo + Juliet, based on Shakespeare's play, reproduced with
permission of Alamy (© Photos 12).

We would like to thank Jackie Murphy for her invaluable help
in the preparation of this book.

Every effort has been made to contact copyright holders of
material reproduced in this book. Any omissions will be
rectified in subsequent printings if notice is given to the
publisher.

Author

Elizabeth Raum writes books for young readers.
She used to teach Shakespeare's plays *Julius Caesar*
and *Romeo and Juliet*, and still finds evidence of
Shakespeare and his plays wherever she goes.

Literacy consultant

Jackie Murphy is Director of Arts at a centre
of teaching and learning. She works with teachers,
artists, and school leaders internationally.

Contents

Some words are printed in bold, **like this**. You can find out
what they mean by looking in the glossary on page 30.

Shakespeare today

Have you ever heard someone say any of the following things?

"He won't *budge an inch*."

"She disappeared *into thin air*."

"It was a *sorry sight*."

"He has *eaten me out of house and home*."

"*Nothing will come of nothing*."

If you have, then you've been listening to words from William Shakespeare. We all use words and phrases in everyday speech that Shakespeare first wrote down about 400 years ago. In the 21st century, Shakespeare is still everywhere.

Shakespeare is on television, at the cinema, and on the Internet. His **verses** appear on greetings cards and in advertisements. You can even download a line or two from Shakespeare as a ringtone for your mobile phone.

The planet Uranus has 27 moons. The one pictured here, Ariel, was named after a character from Shakespeare's play *The Tempest*.

Lots of Shakespeare

An Internet search for "William Shakespeare" brings up more than 13 million websites. There is even a home page named after him. But, of course, he did not create this himself, as he died nearly 400 years ago!

This famous bookstore is named after Shakespeare.

Entire libraries and museums are devoted to his work. Shakespeare festivals are held throughout the world.

You can buy Shakespeare mugs, mouse pads, T-shirts, and cuddly toys. His name appears on restaurants and bookshops. There is even a William Shakespeare Pub in Guatemala City, Guatemala. That is around 8,850 kilometres (5,500 miles) from where Shakespeare lived and worked in England.

No matter where you go in the world, Shakespeare has been there or will be there soon. You may not notice at first, but sooner or later you will find a reminder of Shakespeare.

Who was William Shakespeare?

William Shakespeare was a **playwright** born in 1564 in Stratford-upon-Avon, Warwickshire. Little is known about his early life. In 1582, when Shakespeare was 18, he married Anne Hathaway. They had three children: Susanna, Hamnet, and Judith.

This wax model of Shakespeare is on display at Madame Tussaud's Wax Museum in London.

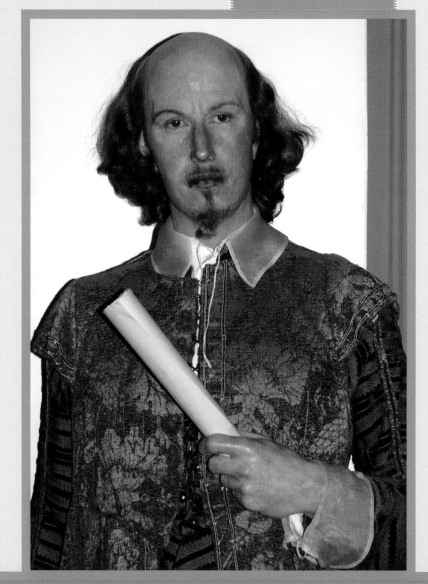

Eventually Shakespeare moved to London (a journey that took three to six days from Stratford at that time) and joined an acting company called Lord Chamberlain's Men. It was later called the King's Men after King James I came to the throne. Shakespeare wrote one or two plays a year for the King's Men. Between 1590 and 1613, he wrote 37 plays and 154 poems. Shakespeare died in 1616, at the age of 52. His works, however, are still alive and well.

Capturing an audience

Shakespeare wrote plays that people wanted to see. His plays include fights of all kinds – with fists, swords, and words. His characters include all sorts of people – kings and clowns, ghosts and witches. In Shakespeare's plays, people fall in love, plan murder, and go mad. They sing, dance, and get married. They moan, take to their beds, and die sad and terrible deaths.

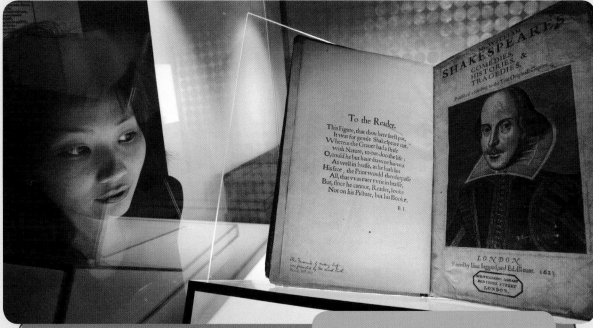

Early copies of Shakespeare's plays are worth millions of pounds today.

Rare and valuable

In 2006 a London book dealer paid £2.8 million for an early copy of Shakespeare's plays called a First **Folio**. (A folio is a large size book.) It was one of 750 copies published in 1623, seven years after Shakespeare died. Two hundred and thirty First Folios still exist. The Folger Shakespeare Library in Washington, D.C., USA, owns 79 First Folios – more than any other library or museum in the world.

Making Shakespeare our own

Today schools, colleges, and community theatres throughout the world perform Shakespeare's plays. Theatre companies such as the Royal Shakespeare Company attract large audiences as do summer Shakespeare festivals. Many Shakespeare festivals are held each year in the UK alone. One festival in Texas, USA, attracted over 450,000 people in just one summer.

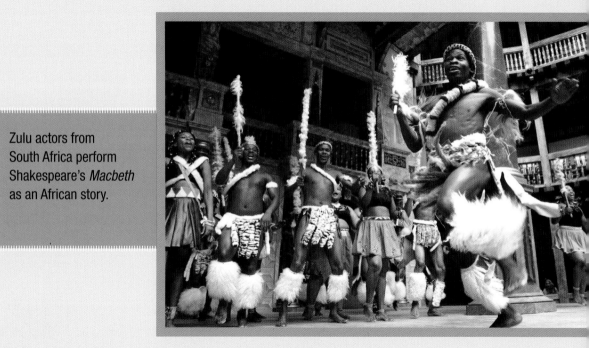

Zulu actors from South Africa perform Shakespeare's *Macbeth* as an African story.

Adapting Shakespeare

Sometimes actors performing Shakespeare use the words and costumes of Shakespeare's day. Others update Shakespeare's language, costumes, and **settings**. Sometimes, in foreign countries, the actors use their native languages and costumes. The Zulu production pictured here shows how people **adapt** (change) Shakespeare to fit their own time and place.

Purépecha Shakespeare

Shakespeare's plays have been translated into hundreds of languages. In 1990 two Mexican writers translated *Hamlet* into the Purépecha language. This language is spoken among the Purépecha people of western Mexico. They performed *Hamlet* using costumes and settings from the Purépecha Empire.

Music and dance

Shakespeare **inspired** (influenced) nearly 300 **operas** (dramatic performances set to music). In the 1800s, the Italian **composer** Giuseppe Verdi wrote *Otello* and *Falstaff* based on Shakespeare's plays. They are among the top 50 operas performed today.

In India actors perform Shakespeare's plays using an Indian form of dance-drama called **Kathakali**. They adapt Shakespeare using Kathakali gestures, body movements, and special make-up.

These Kathakali actors from Kerala, India, tell the story of *King Lear*.

Shakespeare Schools

The Shakespeare Schools Festival began in 2000. Over 75,000 students between the ages of 11 and 18 have performed. Students from over 50 countries participate.

The films

Filmmakers often turn to Shakespeare. Some films are simple versions of the plays. One of the most successful Shakespeare films was *Much Ado About Nothing* (1993), starring Emma Thompson, Kate Beckinsale, and Denzel Washington. It used historical costumes and the language of Shakespeare's time.

Many films, however, adapt Shakespeare for modern audiences. The 1999 film of *A Midsummer Night's Dream*, starring Christian Bale, moves the setting to the late 1800s. *Love's Labour's Lost*, a film made in 2000 starring Alicia Silverstone, turned Shakespeare's play into a 1930s-style musical.

She's the Man, a 2006 film, is based on Shakespeare's *Twelfth Night*. Made for teenage audiences, it takes place in a high school and deals with feelings – such as love and jealousy – that never go out of style.

This film poster for *She's the Man* hints at the complicated story based on Shakespeare's play.

Prince charming

Shakespeare and his work play an important role in the 2004 film *The Prince and Me*, starring Julia Stiles. In this modern fairy tale, a student, Paige, meets a prince, Edvard, from Denmark. Paige tells Edvard that she dislikes Shakespeare, but Edvard knows Shakespeare well. As they get to know each other, they mention the following plays: *Hamlet*, *Macbeth*, *Othello*, *A Midsummer Night's Dream*, and *Romeo and Juliet*.

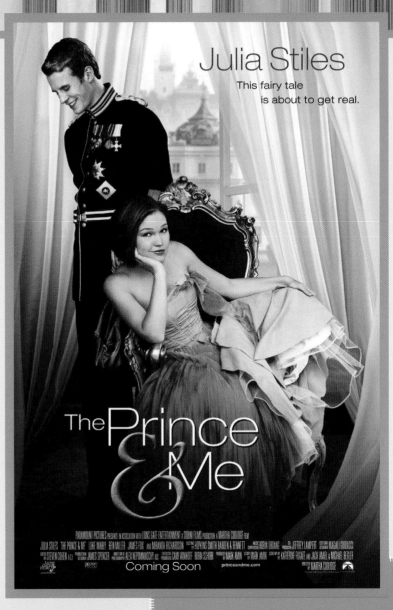

Julia Stiles

This fairy tale is about to get real.

The Prince & Me

Coming Soon   princeandme.com

Viewers of *The Prince & Me* hear many comments about Shakespeare and his plays.

Peter Parker reads Shakespeare

A **scene** in 2004's *Spider-Man 2* shows the books Peter Parker is reading. At the top of the pile is a copy of *Romeo and Juliet*.

A closer look

A closer look at three Shakespearean plays shows the many ways these plays continue to entertain audiences today.

Romeo and Juliet

Several ballets, **operas**, and musicals are based on Shakespeare's *Romeo and Juliet*. Cartoons, advertisements, and films have also been based on the play. *Romeo and Juliet* tells the story of two teenagers in love. Unfortunately, their families hate each other. The families forbid Romeo and Juliet to marry, so they marry in secret. By the end of the play, both Romeo and Juliet are dead.

In 2006 these dancers from the Royal Ballet performed the ballet *Romeo and Juliet*.

Giulietta e Romeo

An Italian-language musical version of *Romeo and Juliet* opened in Verona, Italy, in 2007. The new musical sticks to the original story, but adds modern songs. It even takes place in the real Italian city of Verona, the **setting** for Shakespeare's play. The actors are all between the ages of 15 and 18.

West Side Story

The musical *West Side Story* is based on *Romeo and Juliet*. Two gangs, the Sharks and the Jets, roam the streets of a New York City neighbourhood in the 1950s. When a white boy falls for a Puerto Rican girl, gang warfare results. The musical opened on Broadway in New York in 1957. In 1961 it became a film. In 2009 it returned to Broadway. In the new version, the Puerto Rican characters speak Spanish. Everyone else speaks modern-day English.

In 2008 these New York City performers danced in a scene from *West Side Story*.

Performing Shakespeare

Steps to follow:

1. Read the lines below. Think about the words. What do they mean? In this **scene**, Juliet talks to Romeo from a balcony above a garden. They are in love and have agreed to marry. Juliet promises to send a messenger to Romeo to find out what plans he has made for their wedding. How do you think they feel when they part?

Original language	Modern language
JULIET: Romeo!	Romeo!
ROMEO: My nyas?	My dear?
JULIET: At what o'clock tomorrow shall I send to thee?	What time should I send a messenger to you tomorrow?
ROMEO: By the hour of nine.	Nine o'clock.
JULIET: I will not fail: 'tis twenty year till then. I have forgot why I did call thee back.	I won't fail. It will seem like 20 years until then. I forgot why I called you back.
ROMEO: Let me stand here till thou remember it.	Let me stand here until you remember.
JULIET: I shall forget, to have thee still stand there, rememb'ring how I love thy company.	I will forget so that you will continue to stand there while I remember how much I love your company.
Romeo and Juliet (**Act** 2, Scene 2)	

2. Practise reading the lines. Remember you are acting. Read with emotion. Try to sound as if you mean what you are saying.

3. Shakespeare set this scene in an orchard. But you can change the setting if you like. Will your play take place in the past, today, or the future? Where do Romeo and Juliet live? Think of reasons why their families hate one another. Be creative as you set the scene.

4. Create simple costumes to match your setting. You can ask your audience to imagine the **scenery**, but you will need to describe it for them.

5. Perform your version of this scene for friends and family.

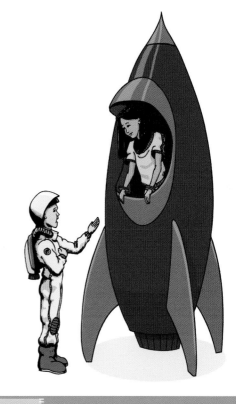

These children have chosen a future setting for their version of *Romeo and Juliet*.

Leonardo DiCaprio and Claire Danes starred in a 1996 film version of *Romeo and Juliet*.

Too old?

In a 1936 U.S. film of *Romeo and Juliet*, the actor playing the teenage Romeo was 43 years old and the actress playing Juliet was 34. In the 1996 version, Leonardo DiCaprio, who played Romeo, was only 22. His Juliet, Claire Danes, was 17.

The Taming of the Shrew

Unlike *Romeo and Juliet*, *The Taming of the **Shrew*** has a happy ending. Katherina and Bianca are sisters. Many men want to marry Bianca, the younger sister. But Katherina scares men away. They consider her a shrew (a scolding, quarrelsome woman). Since Bianca cannot marry until Katherina does, anyone wanting to marry Bianca must find a way to "tame", or soften, Katherina.

Shakespeare quotes

In *A Midsummer Night's Dream*, Shakespeare wrote: "The course of true love never did run smooth" (**Act** 1, Scene 1). The statement is equally true of *The Taming of the Shrew*.

10 Things I Hate About You

Julia Stiles and Heath Ledger starred in *10 Things I Hate About You*, released in 1999. The film, set in a modern secondary school, is based on *The Taming of the Shrew*. Bianca wants a date for the **prom**.

Heath Ledger and Julia Stiles starred in the 1999 film *10 Things I Hate About You.*

Her father will not let her go to the prom unless her older sister, Kat, has a date, too. But who will date Kat? In the film Kat is bright and strong-willed. Bianca is more concerned with popularity.

Animated Shakespeare

The Taming of the Shrew is included in *Shakespeare: The Animated Tales*. In 1994 this cartoon series appeared on television, eventually airing in over 50 countries. The idea began in Wales. The United States and Japan provided money, and Russian artists created the drawings.

This is a production of the musical *Kiss Me, Kate*, which is based on Shakespeare's *The Taming of the Shrew*.

Hamlet

Hamlet is a complicated story about a man (Hamlet) determined to discover who murdered his father, the king of Denmark. *Hamlet* is the longest of Shakespeare's plays. A 1996 film version lasted for four hours. Staged versions have lasted even longer.

The 2006 Chinese film *Ye yan* ("The Banquet") is roughly based on the Hamlet story. *Ye yan* is set in China during the 900s and features beautiful costumes and scenery from that time.

Actor Mark Rylance, playing Hamlet, speaks to Yorick's skull.

Yorick

One of the best-known characters in Hamlet is a skull. Hamlet lifts it up and says, "Alas, poor Yorick. I knew him, Horatio" (Act 5, Scene 1). Yorick was the court **jester** (comedian) who entertained Hamlet when he was a boy. A live Yorick never appears in the play — only his skull does.

An international favourite

Hamlet is popular worldwide. Films based on this play have been made in Turkey, India, Brazil, and Ghana, as well as in Europe and the United States. *Hamlet* has long been popular in Japan. In 2002, France, Great Britain, and Japan joined together to produce a 134-minute film, *The Tragedy of Hamlet*.

The Lion King

This animated film, loosely based on *Hamlet*, set in Africa, features Simba, a lion cub, who must find the truth about the death of his father, Mufasa, the lion king. The popular film became a Broadway musical in 1997 and is still touring the world. In 2007 it reached Africa, playing in Johannesburg, South Africa.

The Lion King continues to entertain audiences both as a film and a stage show.

Shakespeare in cartoons

By 2009 there were hundreds of **graphic novels** based on Shakespeare. Graphic novels use drawings to help the reader understand the story.

Hamlet and *Romeo and Juliet* were the first of Shakespeare's plays to appear as **manga**. Manga are Japanese-style comics. Most manga use Shakespeare's words in new **settings**. For example, a manga version of *Romeo and Juliet* takes place in modern-day Tokyo among rival crime families.

Finding Shakespeare funny

Cartoon strips such as *Peanuts* sometimes mention Shakespeare. The cartoonists expect that readers know something about Shakespeare. In a 1994

This manga version of *Romeo and Juliet* was published in 2007.

Peanuts cartoon, Peppermint Patty stands in front of the class and begins her report: "This is my report on Hamlet … A hamlet is a small village with a population of maybe a few hundred, and … Ma'am?" It's funny because readers know that the teacher expected a report on Shakespeare's play, but the word *hamlet* can also mean a small village.

Create your own Shakespeare cartoon

Steps to follow:

1. Read the quotations below:

   - "If music be the food of love, play on." – *Twelfth Night* (**Act** 1, **Scene** 1)

   - "All the world's a stage, and all the men and women merely players."
     – *As You Like It* (Act 2, Scene 7)

   - "A horse! A horse! My kingdom for a horse!" – *Richard III* (Act 5, Scene 4)

   - "O, beware, my lord, of jealousy; it is the green-eyed monster. . ."
     – *Othello* (Act 3, Scene 3)

   - "How sharper than a serpent's tooth it is to have a thankless child!"
     – *King Lear* (Act 1, Scene 4)

2. Select the quotation you like best. As you read it over, ask yourself these questions:

   - What pictures pop into your head?

   - Where is this scene taking place?

   - Who is speaking? Who is listening?

   - What are they doing?

3. Study the cartoon on this page, and then try drawing your own cartoon to illustrate the quotation you chose. Keep the drawing simple. Use stick figures if you want. Then add colour.

4. Share your cartoon with your friends and family. Can they guess which quotation you chose?

The saying "he has eaten me out of house and home" comes from the second part of Shakespeare's *Henry IV* (Act 2, Scene 1).

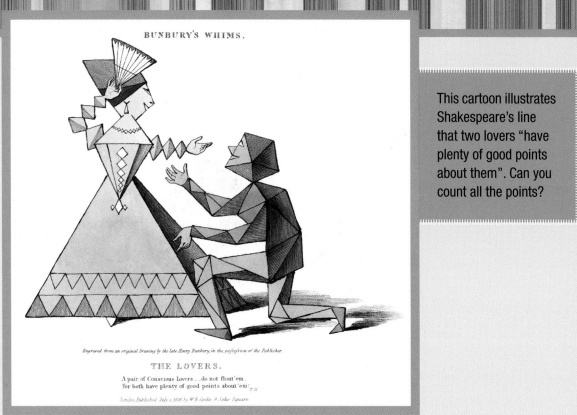

BUNBURY'S WHIMS.

Engraved from an original Drawing by the late Henry Bunbury, in the possession of the Publisher.

THE LOVERS.

A pair of Conscious Lovers — do not flout 'em.
For both have plenty of good points about 'em! *T. H.*

London, Published July 1, 1828, by W.B. Cooke, 9 Soho Square.

This cartoon illustrates Shakespeare's line that two lovers "have plenty of good points about them". Can you count all the points?

Joking around

Comedians use Shakespeare in their performances – holding up a skunk, for example, instead of a skull, and repeating Hamlet's line: "Alas, poor Yorick! I knew him, Horatio." People who know Shakespeare laugh at such jokes. People joke about Shakespeare on television, in live shows, and in written articles.

Speedy Shakespeare

The Reduced Shakespeare Company began in the United States in 1981. The actors perform a shortened version of all 37 plays in 97 minutes. A Reduced Shakespeare Company show is fast-paced and fun. In 2001 the Reduced Shakespeare Company created a televised version of their performances. They continue to perform in person and on the Internet.

Hip-hop Shakespeare

The Hip-Hop Shakespeare Company, founded in London in 2008, combines **hip-hop** music, **rap**, and Shakespeare. Shakespeare's words have a natural beat that blends well with rap. In rap, someone speaks to a regular beat. Rap uses humour, too. *The Bomb-itty of Errors* is a comic rap version of Shakespeare's *Comedy of Errors* that played in London in 2003.

Klingon Shakespeare

Klingon is an invented language used in the *Star Trek* films and television programmes. In 1996 a Klingon version of *Hamlet* was published. *Much Ado About Nothing* was translated into Klingon in 2003. Experts are currently translating *Macbeth*.

AN EPIC QUEST FOR KNOWLEDGE, POWER, AND SURVIVAL

'SPEARE

IN THE WRONG HANDS, SHAKESPEARE'S STORIES ARE POWERFUL ENOUGH TO UNLEASH AN ANCIENT EVIL ...

NOW THE PROSPEARIANS FACE THEIR GREATEST CHALLENGE ...

RESTORING PEACE TO THE UNIVERSE.

COMING TO YOUR SYSTEM SOON
WWW.CANADIANSHAKESPEARES.CA

The video game *'Speare* teaches literacy skills.

Shakespeare video game

'Speare, a video game based on Shakespeare, was developed in Canada in 2007. Players aged 10 to 15 learn lines from Shakespeare while zapping enemy spaceships that have captured an ancient copy of *Romeo and Juliet*.

Wordy Shakespeare

Zany, *lonely*, *horrid*, and *leapfrog* are just a few of the words first recorded by William Shakespeare. Experts who study language note that he used 17,677 different words in his plays. About one-tenth of them were brand new. Some of the words came from spoken language, but they had never been written down. The word *homicide*, which means "murder", is such a word. Sometimes Shakespeare put together two old words to make something new. *Eyeball* (*eye* plus *ball*) and *watchdog* (*watch* plus *dog*) are examples.

More changes

Language continues to change. When Shakespeare made up the word *eyeball*, he was using it to describe the rounded capsule that forms the eye. Today, we also use *eyeball* as a **verb**, or action word. "To eyeball" something means to study it carefully.

Many modern performances continue to use Shakespeare's original language.

Record-setting changes

An expert in the English language wrote, "Shakespeare's was the period of the most rapid growth of **vocabulary** in the recorded history of the language."

Shakespeare word art

Steps to follow:

1. Use this list of words first recorded by Shakespeare to create funny or unusual sentences. Use at least one word from each column.

2. When you are finished, read all the sentences aloud. Then choose your favourite sentence and draw a picture of it.

3. Show your drawing to family and friends. Post it on the refrigerator or your bedroom wall.

The fashionable alligator swaggered in front of the gloomy puppy-dog. Can you find these words on the chart below?

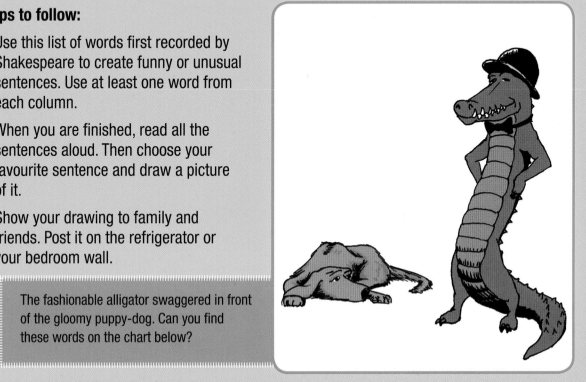

Noun (a person, place, or thing)	Verb (action word)	Adjective (describing word)
alligator	bet	blushing
bandit	cake (to harden)	cold-blooded
bedroom	swagger (to act like a bully)	unreal
bump	puke (to vomit)	deafening
luggage	elbow (to push or prod)	eventful
employer	rant (to talk endlessly)	fashionable
eyeball	undress	flawed (imperfect)
farmhouse	gossip	full-grown
watchdog	hurry	generous
puppy-dog	jig (to sing or dance)	gloomy

Tourist Shakespeare

In Shakespeare's hometown, Stratford-upon-Avon, visitors can tour Shakespeare's birthplace, the house of his wife, Anne Hathaway, and the cemetery where he is buried. The Royal Shakespeare Company performs Shakespeare's plays, and gift shops sell Shakespeare souvenirs.

Tourists also visit the Globe Theatre in London. It was rebuilt in 1997 to look like the original theatre where Shakespeare's plays were performed. Like the first theatre, the new Globe has no roof. It cannot be used in the winter. People come from all over the world to see performances at the Globe.

This is the house where Shakespeare was born. It is open to tourists.

The Globe Theatre in London was opened in 1997.
It is near the site of the original Globe Theatre.

There are Globe Theatres in Rome and the United States. The most unusual one, however, is the Ice Globe Theatre in northern Sweden. It is made of ice. Plays are performed in Sami, the language of the native people of northern Finland, Norway, and Sweden.

At Japan's Shakespeare Country Park near Tokyo, visitors can tour full-size models of Shakespeare's birthplace and other Stratford homes.

Future Shakespeare

The year 2016 will be the 400th anniversary of Shakespeare's death. Celebrations will include new film and musical versions of the plays, video games, and special festivals. We will continue to enjoy Shakespeare in many forms throughout the 21st century.

Shakespeare said

The lines and phrases that Shakespeare wrote 400 years ago are still quoted today. Here are some of Shakespeare's most quoted lines.

"All that glisters [glitters] is not gold."
– *The Merchant of Venice* (**Act** 2, **Scene** 7)

"… be not afraid of greatness. Some are born great, some achieve greatness, and some have greatness thrust upon 'em."
– *Twelfth Night* (Act 2, Scene 5)

"'Tis not enough to help the feeble up, but to support him after."
– *Timon of Athens* (Act 1, Scene 1)

"Friends, Romans, countrymen, lend me your ears."
– *Julius Caesar* (Act 3, Scene 2)

"How poor are they that have not patience!"
– *Othello* (Act 2, Scene 3)

"I have not slept one wink."
– *Cymbeline* (Act 3, Scene 4)

"A man can die but once."
– *Henry IV, Part II* (Act 3, Scene 2)

"The miserable have no other medicine but only hope."
— *Measure for Measure* (Act 3, Scene 1)

"Neither a borrower nor a lender be ..."
— *Hamlet* (Act 1, Scene 3)

"Nothing will come of nothing."
— *King Lear* (Act 1, Scene 1)

"O brave new world, that has such people in't."
— *The Tempest* (Act 5, Scene 1)

"These words are razors to my wounded heart."
— *Titus Andronicus* (Act 1, Scene 1)

"This above all, to thine own self be true."
— *Hamlet* (Act 1, Scene 3)

"To be, or not to be: that is the question."
— *Hamlet* (Act 3, Scene 1)

Glossary

act one of the main divisions of a play or opera

adapt change to fit new circumstances. People adapt Shakespeare's plays to be set in modern times.

composer person who writes music

folio book of the largest common size, usually about 38 centimetres (15 inches) in height

graphic novel book in the form of comic strips. Shakespeare's plays have been rewritten as graphic novels.

hip-hop kind of music that combines beats from songs and spoken words

inspire guide or influence. Shakespeare has inspired many filmmakers.

jester comedian who makes people laugh with tricks and jokes

Kathakali a kind of dance-drama in India

manga Japanese comics. Some manga are based on Shakespeare.

opera play having most of its words set to music

playwright someone who writes plays. William Shakespeare was a playwright.

prom formal dance party, especially one at school or college

rap music that features someone speaking to a regular beat. Hip-hop artist Akala performs Shakespeare as rap music.

scene segment of an act of a play. Shakespeare's plays have many scenes.

scenery backdrops, hangings, furnishings, and other accessories on a stage that represent the location of a scene. There was not much scenery at the Globe Theatre.

setting time and place of a story or play

shrew quarrelsome woman with a violent temper. One of Shakespeare's plays is about changing a shrew into a kind, gentle woman.

verb part of speech that expresses action

verse poem, or piece of poetry

vocabulary body of words used in a particular language

Find out more

Books

The Life and Times of William Shakespeare, Ari Berk and Kristen McDermott (Templar Publishing, 2010)

So You Think You Know Shakespeare?, Clive Gifford (Hodder, 2007)

What's So Special About Shakespeare?, Michael Rosen (Walker, 2007)

Websites

Shakespeare's biography
www.bbc.co.uk/history/historic_figures/shakespeare_william.shtml
Learn about Shakespeare's life on this website.

Shakespeare's quotes
www.shakespeareidentity.co.uk/shakespeares-famous-quotes/
Find out how Shakespeare has affected our language today.

Shakespeare facts
www.bbc.co.uk/coventry/features/local-history/history-view-shakespeare-biography.shtml
Find out lots of facts about Shakespeare.

Places to visit

Shakespeare's Globe Theatre
21 New Globe Walk
Bankside
London SE1 9DT
www.shakespeares-globe.org

Shakespeare's birthplace
Henley Street
Stratford upon Avon
Warwickshire CV37 6QW
www.shakespeare.org.uk

Index